NAME:

USERNAME:

AGE:

EGMONT

We bring stories to life

First published in Great Britain 2013
by Egmont UK Limited
The Yellow Building, 1 Nicholas Road,
London W11 4AN

Edited by Jane Riordan.
Designed by Steffan Glynn with help from Tiffany Leeson and Maddox Philpot.
Illustrated by James Burlinson and Steffan Glynn.
Written by Jane Riordan, Stephanie Milton, Nick Farwell and Paul Soares Jr.
With thanks to the Minecraft testing crew: Laurids Binderup, Sam Foxall,
Adam, William, Charlie, Parsa, Luca, Robert, Max, Petros, Jack, Gethin, Luke, Isaac and Oscar.

'Minecraft' is a trademark of Notch Development AB

ISBN 978 1 4052 6767 0
55152/17
Printed in Italy

Stay safe online. Any website addresses listed in this book are correct at the time of going to print. However, Egmont is not responsible for content hosted by third parties. Please be aware that online content can be subject to change and websites can contain content that is unsuitable for children. We advise that all children are supervised when using the internet.

The publishers have used every endeavour to trace copyright owners and secure appropriate permissions for materials reproduced in this book. In case of any unintentional omission, the publishers will be pleased to hear from the relevant copyright owner.

MINECRAFT™

ANNUAL 2014

MOJANG

Contents

THIS IS MINECRAFT
THE MOJANG LOWDOWN   8
GETTING STARTED   12
MOBESTIARY   14
BLOCKS   18
TOOL BAR   20
BIOMES   22
MY MINECRAFT   26

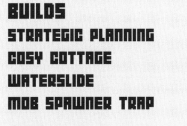

BUILDS
STRATEGIC PLANNING   28
COSY COTTAGE   30
WATERSLIDE   34
MOB SPAWNER TRAP   38

REDSTONE
SLIDING PISTON DOOR   42

PAPERCRAFT
DESIGN YOUR OWN SKINS   46
BUILD YOUR OWN DIRT BLOCK   48
CRAFT YOUR OWN CREEPER   49

PUZZLES AND GAMES
SPIDER WEB   50
KNOCK KNOCK   51
CODE BREAKING   53
SSSS ... BOOM!   54
MINECRAFT MAPPING   56
A-MAZE-ING   58
RIDE THE PIG   60
BLOCK-BUSTER   62

FINAL WORDS FROM JEB   64
ANSWERS   66
READER SURVEY   67

THE MOJANG LOWDOWN

MOJANG AB

Mojang Aktiebolag, translates into English as Gadget Ltd.

WHO?

At the time of writing, Mojang has a team of 32, including business folk, games developers, web developers and artists.

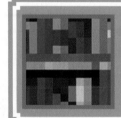

DID YOU KNOW?

Mojang's HQ in Stockholm has an entire wall covered in Victorian-style portraits of every member of the team.

FOUNDERS

Markus Alexej Persson
AKA

NOTCH

Co-founder of Mojang and creator of Minecraft. Notch was born in Stockholm, Sweden, in 1979. He started programming at the age of 7 and wrote his first game at the age of 8. He worked for two game companies in Sweden before founding Mojang. He has now handed over control of Minecraft development to Jens Bergensten and is currently working on a new game for Mojang. And just in case you needed proof that he's a smart guy, he's a member of Mensa Sweden.

Team Fortress 2 is one of his favourite games but he loves pinball and board games, too. If you manage to kill him in-game, he drops an apple! He's the only player in the whole of Minecraft who does this.

Jakob Porsér

Co-founder of Mojang and game developer. He worked with Notch prior to Mojang and they teamed up again when Minecraft started to gain popularity. He is currently the lead developer behind Scrolls. He is an avid supporter of the Luleå ice hockey team.

Carl Manneh

Co-founder of Mojang and the Chief Executive Officer. He previously ran jAlbum and was brought to Mojang to run the business side of the company. Carl is the guy responsible for signing all their top-secret contracts.

THE MINECRAFT TEAM PC/MAC EDITION

Jens Bergensten
AKA
JEB

The lead Minecraft developer, after taking over from Notch in 2012. He made up the name Jeb because he wanted a more English-sounding name to use on the internet. It's a shortened version of Jens Bergensten. He is the ultimate authority on all things Minecraft and is responsible for all recent releases and updates. Pistons and wolves are just two of his legacies. Previously he worked at Oxeye, the game studio responsible for Cobalt.

Nathan Adams
AKA
DINNERBONE

This British developer is a member of the Bukkit team and is also responsible for the development of the mod API. He is red-green colourblind, hence his favourite colour is blue.

Erik Broes
AKA
GRUM

Born in Holland, he was originally hired to develop the official plug-in API and to maintain the Minecraft server. He is now involved in general game development. His Minecraft skin is the character Elmo!

9

XBOX 360 EDITION

4J Studios

Based in East Linton and Dundee, this Scottish video game development studio have worked on many high-profile games, most notably the Xbox 360 Edition of Minecraft. In 2012 they won a TIGA Games Industry Award for Best Arcade Game for Minecraft.

The Xbox 360 Edition has sold over 7 million copies since it was first released in May 2012. When the disc-based Xbox 360 Edition was released in 2013, it was the fastest-selling console game in the US.

POCKET EDITION

Aron Nieminen

This game developer was integral to the creation of the Pocket Edition. He led all versions from the prerelease to Alpha 0.3.2. After this version he continued to work on the Pocket Edition alongside Johan. Rumour has it that he's the best pinball player at the Mojang HQ!

Johan Bernhardsson

Credited with many of the recent updates to the Pocket Edition, this Swedish game developer has been working at Mojang since early 2012. Among other things he is responsible for adding beds, bows and, a little more recently, bringing Minecraft Realms to the Pocket Edition.

Daniel Kaplan
AKA
KAPPISCHE

The first employee to join Mojang, he has worked across many different products but is currently focused on the Xbox 360 Edition. His official title is business developer, but he does a lot more than just business stuff. He handles communication between Apple, Google, Microsoft, 4J Studios and lots more ... He does an excellent impression of Link from the Zelda games. He is also one of the founders of www.ludosity.com.

MOJANG

WHERE?

Stockholm, Sweden.

WHEN?

Mojang was founded in May 2009.
Notch left his day job to work on Minecraft full-time in June 2009.

WHAT?

An independent Swedish video game developer, most famous for creating Minecraft and currently working on the development of the game Scrolls and other projects, while continuing to update Minecraft.

WHY?

When Minecraft started to take off, Notch approached Jakob Porsér and suggested starting an independent company together. Jakob was thrilled by the idea, because it would enable him to concentrate on developing the games he wanted and also give him the chance to work with former colleague Notch again.

Since then the company has grown, but it has always tried to maintain its indie ethos and foster creativity.

GETTING STARTED

You're stranded, alone in a strange new world. Daylight lasts just ten minutes before night falls and monsters come out ... to hunt you down. Now is the time to mine, to craft and to create. These essential tips should help you to stay one step ahead of the hostile mobs during those first few nail-biting nights.

STEVE
This is you, in all your Minecraft-y glory. If you're not happy with your image, you can change it later by uploading a new skin. See page 46 for some skin-spiration!

SHEEP
Cute, isn't it? And you don't have to kill it to get wool. Simply craft yourself a pair of shears (see page 21) and get chopping.

TREE
It may seem strange, but if you want to survive you're going to have to hit the trunk of this tree repeatedly until you get wood.

SUN

Keep an eye on the sun's progress through the sky. Just before nightfall, go into your shelter, shut the door and hope for the best!

BED

Allows you to sleep at night, skipping ahead to the next morning when it's safe to go outside again.

TORCHES

Essential both inside and outside as they prevent hostile mobs from spawning around you.

CHEST

Your inventory can only hold so much. Keep your loot safe in a chest. A small chest has 27 storage slots and a large one has 54.

SHELTER

Without a shelter you are at the mercy of the mobs who come out after dark. Your first shelter can be very simple, just dirt blocks will do.

CRAFTING TABLE

An essential piece of kit, used to craft most of the items in the game, you'll need access to one of these at all times. Set one up in your shelter immediately.

FURNACE

Enables you to cook meat, making it safer and more filling than raw meat. Can also be used to smelt ore and create glass for windows.

WOODEN DOOR

With one of these you'll be safe from hostile mobs, unless you have changed your difficulty to hard. Just don't forget to close it behind you!

MOBESTIARY

PASSIVE MOBS - YOUR FRIENDS!

Meet the mobs (from the word 'mobile') – the living, moving game entities in Minecraft. The mobs you'll find here are all passive or neutral. Neutral means that they aren't a threat to you unless you attack them. Turn the page for their more dangerous cousins!

Mobs are vulnerable to falling, drowning, suffocating and, with some exceptions, to fire. Most mobs drop items when killed, which are often useful resources. These are shown in the small icon boxes.

The heart icons next to each mob show their health points. The higher their health point rating, the harder they are to kill.

STEVE

The generic Minecraft player whose skin can be customised. He is right-handed and his shirt is always left casually untucked on the left-hand side. He is known as Stevie in the Pocket Edition. In the Xbox 360 Edition he's just good old Steve and there are 8 skins to choose from.

VILLAGERS

Spawn and move about in NPC (Non-Player Character) villages. They never leave their village and hide in their houses at night and when it rains. Each villager has a profession – either farmer, priest, butcher, blacksmith or librarian. They like to trade items with players, so pay them a visit.

PIGS

Roam in the Overworld in groups of 3 or 4. When killed they drop pork chops, which are better for you if they are cooked before eating. Pigs can be bred using carrots (PC version) or wheat (Xbox version) and it then takes one full Minecraft day and night for a piglet to grow into an adult pig. Unexpectedly, pigs are a useful mode of transport and can be ridden using a saddle and controlled with a carrot on a stick. When struck by lightning, they turn into zombie pigmen and become hostile if attacked - so beware!

SHEEP

Most commonly white, grey, brown or black, they do occasionally naturally spawn pink! They eat grass, turning it into a dirt block. Lambs eat faster than sheep. Sheep can be dyed with 16 different colours, as shown below, before shearing to produce coloured wool. Wool is needed to craft a bed, which is crucial to the game, and also for decorative items such as paintings and carpets.

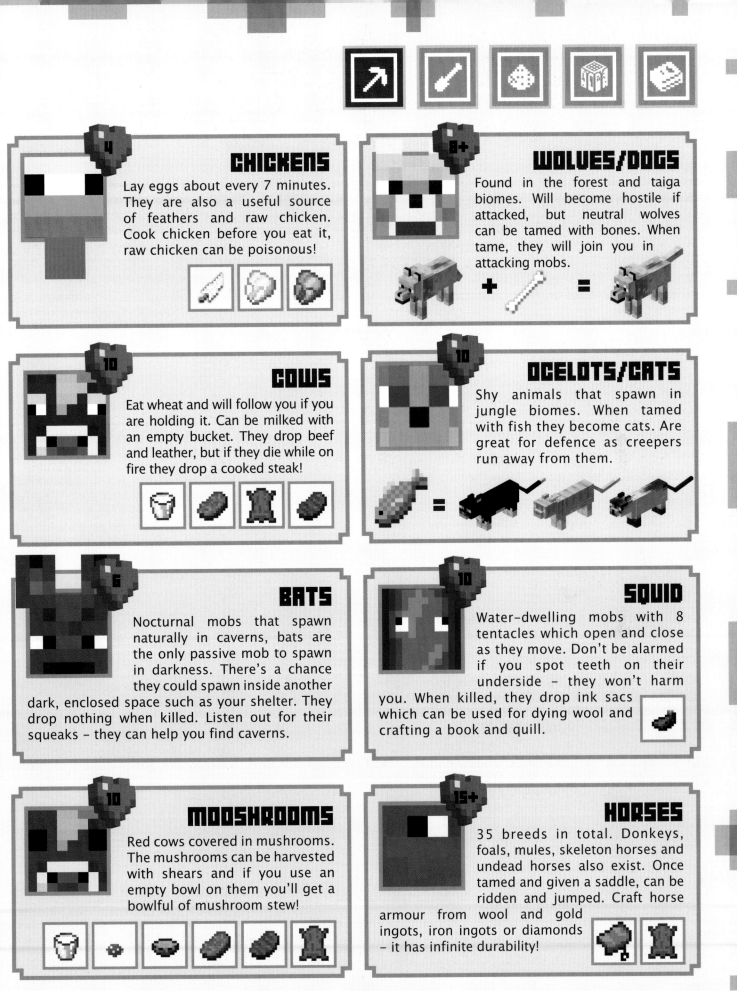

CHICKENS

Lay eggs about every 7 minutes. They are also a useful source of feathers and raw chicken. Cook chicken before you eat it, raw chicken can be poisonous!

WOLVES/DOGS

Found in the forest and taiga biomes. Will become hostile if attacked, but neutral wolves can be tamed with bones. When tame, they will join you in attacking mobs.

COWS

Eat wheat and will follow you if you are holding it. Can be milked with an empty bucket. They drop beef and leather, but if they die while on fire they drop a cooked steak!

OCELOTS/CATS

Shy animals that spawn in jungle biomes. When tamed with fish they become cats. Are great for defence as creepers run away from them.

BATS

Nocturnal mobs that spawn naturally in caverns, bats are the only passive mob to spawn in darkness. There's a chance they could spawn inside another dark, enclosed space such as your shelter. They drop nothing when killed. Listen out for their squeaks - they can help you find caverns.

SQUID

Water-dwelling mobs with 8 tentacles which open and close as they move. Don't be alarmed if you spot teeth on their underside - they won't harm you. When killed, they drop ink sacs which can be used for dying wool and crafting a book and quill.

MOOSHROOMS

Red cows covered in mushrooms. The mushrooms can be harvested with shears and if you use an empty bowl on them you'll get a bowlful of mushroom stew!

HORSES

35 breeds in total. Donkeys, foals, mules, skeleton horses and undead horses also exist. Once tamed and given a saddle, can be ridden and jumped. Craft horse armour from wool and gold ingots, iron ingots or diamonds - it has infinite durability!

MOBESTIARY

HOSTILE MOBS - YOUR FOES!

These guys are less than friendly, and if you encounter them unprepared you'll soon find yourself getting killed. Oh, and don't believe everything you hear about them only coming out at night – it's not quite as simple as that! You'll run into these guys in lots of dark places. The heart icons show each mob's health points and the small icons show what each mob drops.

CREEPERS

The most infamous mob in the game. Creepers have only one goal in life – to explode in your face! They are almost completely silent, but they hiss quietly moments before exploding. They don't catch fire in daylight, making them a constant threat. They spawn in the Overworld at night or anywhere with a light level of 7 or less. Creepers run away from cats and ocelots, so a tame cat makes for a great companion. Creepers drop gunpowder if killed by players and music discs if killed by skeletons.

If lightning strikes a creeper it becomes a charged creeper – an even more explosive version. You can recognise a charged creeper by the blue glow that surrounds it.

SPIDERS

Not hostile in daylight, so you're safe unless night falls or you stumble across them in a dark area such as a cave. Watch out, because these bad guys can climb walls, jump large distances and their glowing red eyes can see you through solid blocks!

ZOMBIES

Slow-moving undead mobs that will attempt to break down your door at night. Don't eat the rotten flesh they drop – there's a good chance it will poison you.

SLIMES

Infuriating creatures that come in three sizes: large, medium or tiny. They hop towards you, inflicting damage when they make contact. When killed they divide and multiply into smaller slimes. Slimeballs dropped by tiny slimes are an essential ingredient for sticky pistons.

SKELETONS

Quick on their feet and armed with bows and arrows, which makes melee/hand-to-hand combat difficult. Give them a taste of their own medicine and use a bow against them from a safe distance.

CAVE SPIDERS

Spawn underground and have a poisonous bite. If bitten, your health will slowly deplete. They will soon outnumber you, so your best defence is to find the spawner they are coming from and either destroy it or disable it by surrounding it with torches.

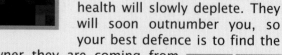

BLAZES

20

Spawn in Nether fortresses and hurl fireballs at you, as well as catching fire randomly. Snowballs damage blazes. Once you've damaged it with snowballs, you can finish the blaze off with your sword. They drop blaze rods, which are used in brewing potions.

MAGMA CUBES

16

Found in the Nether and similar to slimes as they divide and multiply when killed, releasing 2-4 smaller magma cubes. As they move, they stretch out like a spring, revealing their molten lava core. Both large and small drop magma cream, used in making fire resistance potions.

GHASTS

10

Large, ghost-like mobs that float through the Nether, wailing and crying. They shoot fireballs from their mouths, which you can hit with a weapon to deflect them right back at the ghast! Drop gunpowder and ghast tears when killed.

ZOMBIE PIGMEN

20

Half zombie, half pig – the Nether is swarming with these guys. They are harmless until you attack one, and then every zombie pigman in the area will come to their aid and attack you – beware!

WITHER SKELETONS

20

The Nether equivalent of skeletons, they spawn in fortresses and are immune to fire and lava. They wield stone swords and if hit, you'll be inflicted with the 'wither' effect. Drop coal, bones and, rarely, a skull.

SPIDER JOCKEYS

36

What's worse than an agile spider? An agile spider with a bow-wielding skeleton riding it. Fortunately they are rare. Divide and conquer – tackle the skeleton first with a bow and arrows, then go for the spider.

WITCHES

26

Spawn in witch huts and use splash potions as weapons. Their range is shorter than the range of your bow however, so attack them from afar.

ENDERMEN

40

Tall, thin creatures who wander the land at night, moving blocks around. They won't attack you unless you aggravate them, but accidentally catching them in your crosshairs from the legs up will be enough to get them in a rage. They can teleport around, taking you by surprise!

BLOCKS

Believe it or not, there are 153 different blocks in Minecraft, ranging from the mundane such as wood and dirt to the ridiculous like melon and monster spawners. Together they build up the totally unique environment that makes this game so special.

Here are just a few of the blocks you'll come across, with some additional little-known facts to enhance your gameplay.

DIRT

Of limited use. A basic filler block found in abundance in the Overworld. Easily mined, even by hand. Limited uses, although can be used to create a basic shelter in an emergency, if stranded outside at night. Important in crop growing as when you use a hoe on it, it will turn into a block of farmland.

WOOD

Often the first block to be collected, by hitting a tree trunk. A crucial block for crafting many tools and blocks. There are 4 types: oak, birch, spruce and jungle, and each generates within a specific biome. Flammable, so take care. If you can't find coal, burn wood in your furnace to make charcoal.

WATER

A fluid block found at ocean level and also in lakes, underground springs, desert wells, village wells and waterfalls. Carry a bucket of water with you at all times to put out any fires you encounter. When flowing water hits lava source blocks it will form obsidian. There is no water in the Nether.

COAL

Frequently found in cliff faces above ground as well as in caves, this is the only ore that occurs well above sea level. Veins of coal ore can sometimes be up to 64 blocks in size. When mined, coal ore will drop 1 piece of coal. You can combine pieces of coal with sticks to create torches.

SAND

Found in desert biomes and on coasts, sand is easily mineable. It needs to be supported by solid blocks, so when the block below is destroyed, sand will fall until it hits another solid block. Sand is an essential ingredient in gunpowder and can also be smelted in a furnace to produce glass.

SNOW

Crafted from 4 snowballs, snow blocks can be used to build igloos and other snowy structures. Place a pumpkin on top of 2 snow blocks to create a snow golem. If you want your 4 snowballs back, destroy the block with a shovel. Oddly, snow blocks aren't affected by lava, fire or torches!

ICE

Formed from exposed water in icy biomes, ice is a slippery, semi-transparent block. It sits on the top of areas of water, and when broken will revert to water, unless there's no block directly below it. Try using ice blocks at the bottom of a water slide to speed up your ride! Torches can't be placed on ice.

GLASS

A highly useful transparent block, obtained by smelting sand in a furnace. It can be used to make windows to let light into your buildings, and allows you to keep an eye on what's going on outside. It can also be used to make glass bottles which are useful in brewing potions.

GRAVEL

Found in pits, underwater, on beaches, in NPC villages as pathways and in the Nether. Gravel is a solid block that is affected by gravity and will fall when the block below it is removed. When mined using a shovel, there's a 10% chance gravel will drop flint, which can be used to make arrows or a flint and steel.

MELON

Grown from melon seeds, can be destroyed to produce melon slices which restore 2 hunger points. You can also build structures from melon blocks. Make your own melon farm by hunting down melon seeds in an abandoned mineshaft chest, or getting melon slices through villager trading.

PUMPKIN

A rare block found on grassy areas in mountains and plains. Pumpkins can be used to craft an iron golem, a Jack 'o' lantern or a pumpkin pie. They can also be worn as a helmet. This won't protect you from attack, but it will allow you to look at an enderman without it becoming hostile.

GLOWSTONE

Found in the Nether, glowstone has a higher light level than torches and will glow indefinitely. When mined, a block of glowstone will drop 2-4 pieces of glowstone dust, which can then be rebuilt into blocks of glowstone. You can sometimes get glowstone through villager trading.

REDSTONE ORE

A valuable ore that has magnetic and conductive properties and is used in circuitry. Regularly found within 10 blocks of the bedrock layer but also at higher elevations, one block will drop 4-5 redstone dust when mined with an iron pickaxe or better. Veins of redstone ore will likely be 4-8 blocks in size.

DIAMOND ORE

A rare and valuable ore found within 16 blocks of the bedrock layer (although not as rare as emerald ore). When mined, will give you a diamond that can be used to craft the strongest armour and weapons, as well as enchanting tables and jukeboxes. Veins of diamond ore are usually 4-8 blocks in size.

OBSIDIAN

Formed when flowing water hits lava, obsidian is highly durable and the sole block that can only be mined with a diamond pickaxe. Obsidian is a necessary ingredient in crafting Nether portals, ender chests and enchanting tables, and a good material to build a shelter from as it is so strong.

TOOL BAR

whilst all players begin digging by hand, it won't be long before you will want to create some tools to speed up your mining, not to mention acquiring all those materials that just aren't possible to mine by hand. Tools will become damaged over time with use, but happily they can be repaired by simply placing two items of the same type and material on the crafting grid. This will result in a single repaired item with increased durability.

PICKAXE

There are 5 types of pickaxe: wood, stone, iron, gold and diamond. Pickaxes are required to mine all ores and many other types of blocks. The crafting table here shows how pickaxes can be made but they also occur naturally, sometimes spawning inside chests in abandoned mineshafts, strongholds and village blacksmiths. Only a diamond pickaxe can mine obsidian, and diamond and emerald can only be harvested with iron or diamond pickaxes.

SHOVEL

Essential to collect snowballs from snow, but otherwise they simply make the collection of blocks such as dirt, sand, gravel and clay easier – blocks which can also be collected by hand. Shovels are also needed to get flint from gravel. Gold shovels work faster than any other type but are not at all durable. It is very rare, but occasionally zombies drop an iron shovel when killed. Diamond shovels win overall on speed of block destruction and durability.

AXE

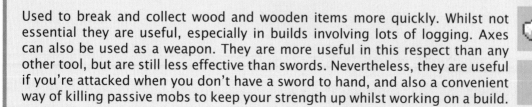

Used to break and collect wood and wooden items more quickly. Whilst not essential they are useful, especially in builds involving lots of logging. Axes can also be used as a weapon. They are more useful in this respect than any other tool, but are still less effective than swords. Nevertheless, they are useful if you're attacked when you don't have a sword to hand, and also a convenient way of killing passive mobs to keep your strength up whilst working on a build.

Crafting is trickiest on a PC or a Mac. The Xbox and Pocket Editions tell you what you can make with the items you have.

COMPASS

Usefully, the needle points to the player's spawn point. Compasses don't work in the Nether, however. Also used in crafting maps.

CLOCK

Shows the sun and the moon's position in relation to the horizon. Useful in mines, and also for knowing the earliest opportunity to sleep.

FISHING ROD

Used for obtaining raw fish for food or taming. When fishing, the line must be reeled in as soon as the bobber disappears below the surface of the water.

SHEARS

Used to shear sheep for wool, get string from cobwebs, harvest red mushrooms, as well as removing tripwires and harvesting many types of plants.

FLINT AND STEEL

Places a block of fire which can then be used to ignite TNT, destroy flammable blocks or as a way of attacking hostile mobs.

MAP

Allows the player to see the area they have explored, updating itself constantly. The scale can be increased by adding paper on a crafting table.

BUCKET

When used on a source block can carry water or lava. Can carry milk when used on a cow or mooshroom. Can create underwater air pockets.

CARROT ON A STICK

Once a pig is saddled this tool can be used to control its direction. The pig will eat the carrot, so it will have to be rebuilt after time.

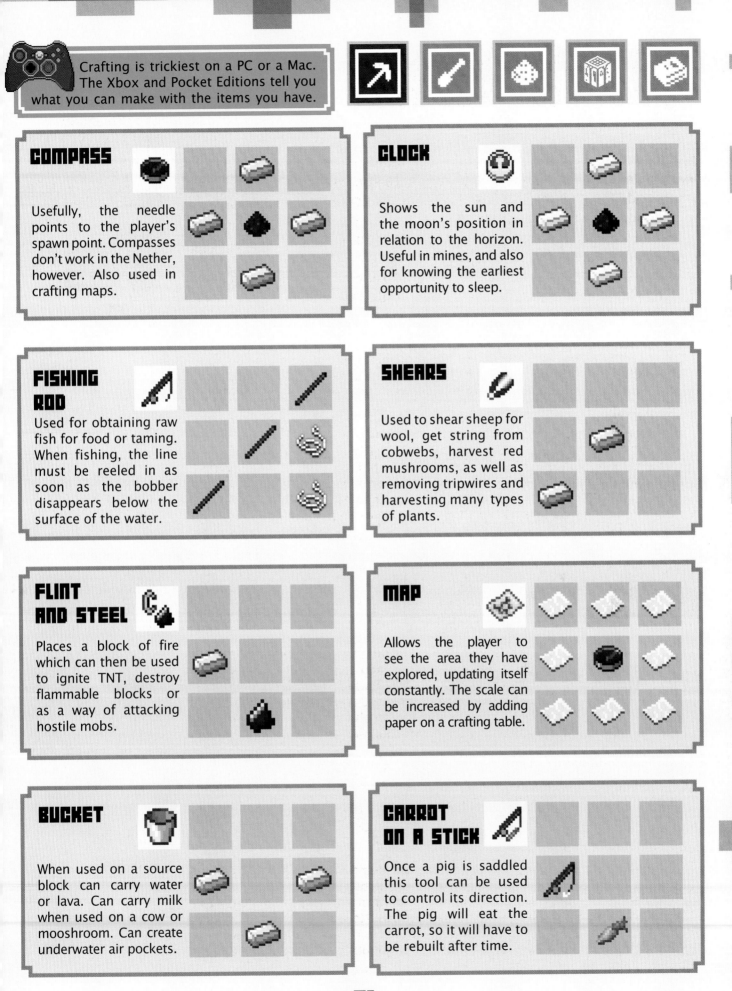

BIOMES

A biome is a particular type of landscape or ecosystem in Minecraft. There are 10 main types of biomes in the Overworld.

PLAINS

A flat landscape without many trees but with long grasses. NPC villages, such as the one pictured on the left, waterholes and gullies are common in this biome.

FOREST

Filled with grass and trees, a great biome to start out in as it provides all the wood you'll need, but it is particularly dangerous at night!

EXTREME HILLS

The best biome for views with its mountains, ledges, waterfalls and floating islands. Also characterised by many cave systems.

OCEAN

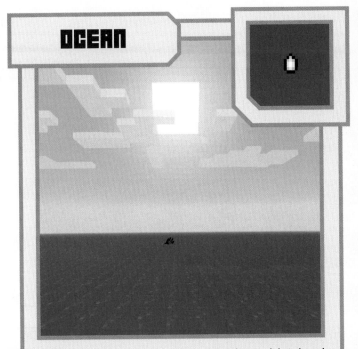

Vast expanses of water with the odd island dotted around. You can find some interesting features underwater, if you're brave enough to venture down there.

SWAMPLAND

Flat land interspersed with shallow pools of water, with floating lily pads and trees growing out of the water. Mushrooms and sugar cane can be found in this biome.

DESERT

Barren landscapes where rain never falls and little can be found other than sand, cacti and dead bushes.

Very rarely, desert wells can be found which provide an infinite water source, which is particularly valued in this harsh biome.

Deserts aren't much fun unless you stumble upon a desert temple. Inside the main chamber there are several squares of orange wool in the floor, and one block of blue wool. Underneath this block of blue wool is a secret chamber filled with chests full of valuable items. But beware – the chamber is booby-trapped with pressure plates connected to TNT, so you'll need to find a way of getting to the chests without activating the traps, or …

KABOOM!

BIOMES CONTINUED

JUNGLE

A dense, tropical biome full of giant jungle trees (sometimes reaching up to 31 blocks high), ferns, vines, regular oak trees and some low level bushes. The landscape is lush, green and hilly, and you'll be able to spot small, picturesque lakes every so often between the tall trees.

Ocelots only appear in the jungle biome. If caught, they can be tamed and kept as pets. Just approach one carefully whilst holding raw fish and feed it to them.

And if you have a sweet tooth, the jungle is the place to go to find cocoa pods which can be harvested and combined with wheat to make delicious chocolate chip cookies.

DID YOU KNOW?

As well as containing chests with possible treasure in, jungle temples also contain traps – so take care!

TAIGA

A hilly biome characterised by its spruce trees. Snow falls in this biome and ice is common. You can often spot wolves here, which can be tamed with bones to become loyal dogs.

TUNDRA

A flat, snowy landscape with frozen lakes and rivers. It doesn't rain in this biome, it snows instead. This is a particularly difficult biome to survive in due to the scarcity of wood.

MUSHROOM

A very rare biome covered with huge mushrooms and mycelium (this biome's equivalent of grass). It's a mixture of flat landscape and hills, and is usually on an ocean island.

The only mob that spawns naturally here is the mooshroom, which means you'll get some peace from hostile mobs. Mooshrooms can be sheared to collect mushrooms, and using a bowl on them will give you mushroom stew.

Trees and other dirt and grass-based plants can be grown from saplings, as long as they aren't directly adjacent to mycelium, which will take over the dirt square from the plant and uproot it. Mycelium can't be tilled. You'll need to dig it up and replace it with dirt which can be tilled. Once created, farmland will resist takeover by mycelium.

MY MINECRAFT

STATS, FACTS AND FAVES..

USERNAME:

DATE I JOINED MINECRAFT:

PREFERRED GAMEPLAY MODE:

TOP SERVER:

FAVOURITE MINECRAFT YOUTUBER:

MOST FEARED MOB:

WEIRDEST EXPERIENCE IN MINECRAFT:

MY MINECRAFT SKIN

BEST PERSONAL BUILD:

TICK THESE AS YOU FIND THEM

VILLAGE ☐

SADDLE ☐

MELON SEEDS ☐

MOB SPAWNER ☐

ABANDONED MINESHAFT ☐

WITCH HUT ☐

DESERT TEMPLE ☐

JUNGLE TEMPLE ☐

STRONGHOLD ☐

DIAMOND ☐

EMERALD ☐

THE NETHER ☐

NETHER FORTRESS ☐

MUSHROOM BIOME ☐

THE END ☐

DRAGON EGG ☐

BEST MOMENT

STRATEGIC PLANNING

So, you've got the Mojang lowdown, been warned about the hostile mobs and made it through your first night, now it's time to get stuck into some serious building. The best construction projects need a plan.

We're showing off and have created a blueprint in Minecraft for a cosy cottage using snow and blue wool, but a rough design using pen and paper will do the trick … just don't spill your drink on it!

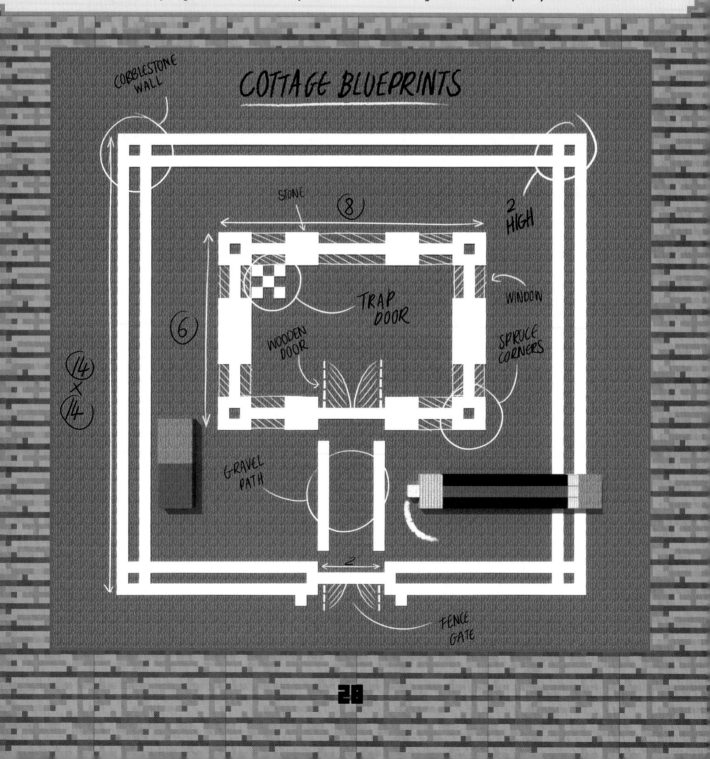

COTTAGE BLUEPRINTS

COBBLESTONE WALL

STONE

8

2 HIGH

WINDOW

SPRUCE CORNERS

TRAP DOOR

6

WOODEN DOOR

14 X 14

GRAVEL PATH

2

FENCE GATE

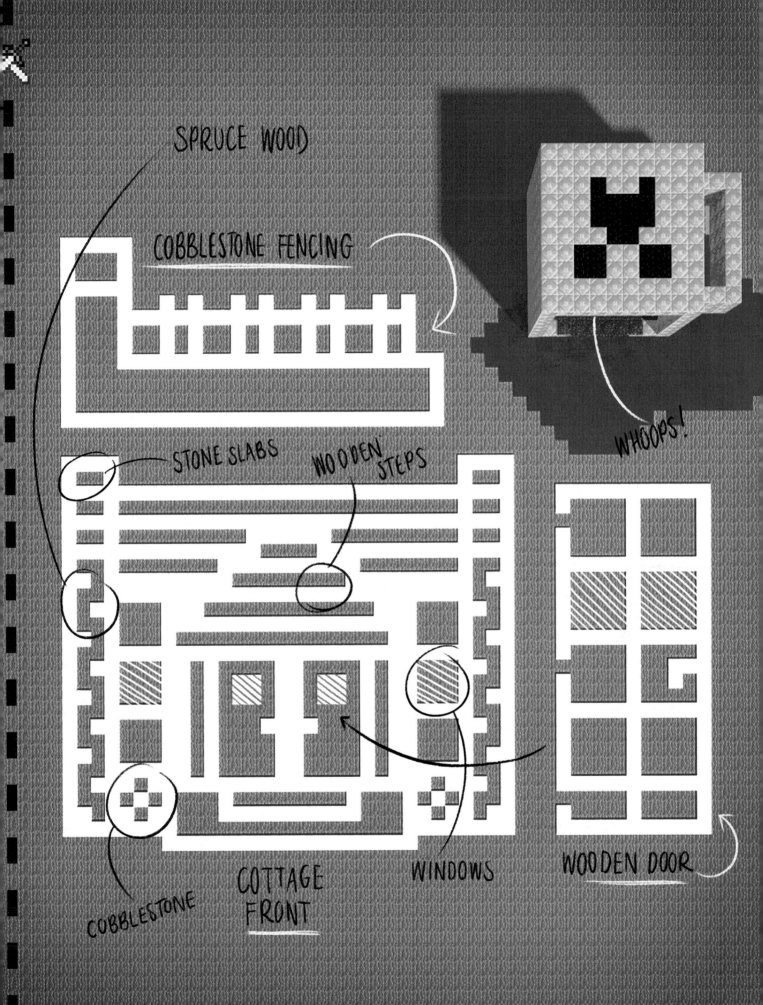

SPRUCE WOOD

COBBLESTONE FENCING

WHOOPS!

STONE SLABS

WOODEN STEPS

WINDOWS

WOODEN DOOR

COBBLESTONE

COTTAGE FRONT

MINECRAFT

HOW TO BUILD A
COSY COTTAGE

DIFFICULTY ■ □ □

It's a really dangerous world out there, so you're going to want a cosy base to call your own – safe from spiders, creepers, skeletons and zombies. Here's how to build your very own safe place – your refuge.

BY PAUL SOARES JR

Paul Soares Jr is a Minecraft expert and was the first person to make Minecraft tutorials for YouTube. Check out his channel for more pro tips!

YOUTUBE.COM/PAULSOARESJR

CONSTRUCTION MATERIALS

32	64	4	64	64	
64	32	64	64	18	16
2	2	10	6	1	8

1

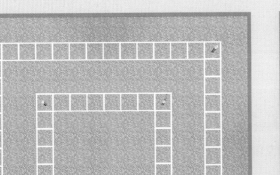

In terms of location, you'll need a flat, clear area. Using torches, mark the corners of the security wall (14 x 14) and the cottage (8 x 6).

With your shovel, start digging the 8 x 6 area for the foundation. Dig down three blocks deep. Watch out for pitfalls!

i

HOW TO BUILD A COSY COTTAGE

2

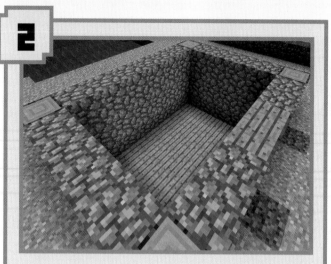

Use cobblestone to build the basement walls and oak wood planks for the flooring. Then use more cobblestone to construct the foundation wall one block high and use spruce wood for the four corners. You can also mark out a doorway with the planks.

3

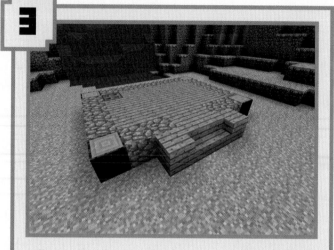

Fill in the floor with oak wood planks and install the trapdoor to the basement in the corner. Finally, use oak wood planks and two oak wood stairs for the front step. Hungry yet? This might be a good time to take a break and eat a snack!

4

Place spruce wood to raise the corners 4 blocks high. Build the cottage walls using stone bricks. You remembered to leave spaces for the windows? Good! Now put in the glass panes and the doors. Use stairs and fences for the front-entry overhang.

5

Use spruce wood to raise the corner frames up one more block. Lay stone bricks to fill the gaps between the frames on the two sides. Use oak wood stairs to cover the stone bricks at the front and back. Finally, fill in the ceiling with oak wood planks.

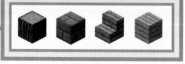

6

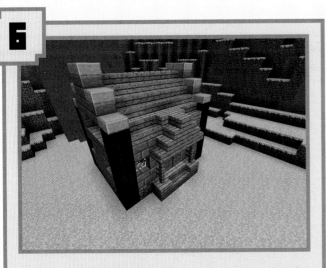

Build up the roof supports using stone bricks and for a really smart finish cap them off with stone slabs. And now it's time to raise the roof using oak wood stairs to form a peak along the centre of the cottage. Be careful not to slip on that roof and fall!

7

Step back and admire your work! Looks great, doesn't it, but you don't want monsters knocking on your door and peeking in your windows, do you? No, of course not! So let's build a wall all the way around the cottage to keep those hostile mobs well away.

8

Using the outer torch markings, lay down a cobblestone wall with front gateposts. Place wooden fences on the wall and cap the corners and gateposts with stone slabs. Install a pair of fence gates and perhaps a gravel path to your cottage.

9

No home is complete without furniture, decorations and landscaping, so go ahead and add some charm and comfort to your cosy cottage. Here we've got seating built out of stairs, a shelf of books, flowers and even a rug on the floor!

HOW TO BUILD A
WATERSLIDE
BY PAUL SOARES JR

In the mood for some water sport? Here's a simple guide to building your own waterslide. The best part is that it can be as long as you want! You could even make one that turns corners or goes through mountains – the options are limitless. So where will your imagination take you?

CONSTRUCTION MATERIALS

DID YOU KNOW?
If heights make you nervous, you can use the sneak function when standing on the edges of your slide. This will stop you from falling off.

1

Begin by finding a relatively flat area next to water. Build a platform with wooden planks right above the edge of the water. Make sure the water is at least 3 blocks deep and check there's nothing for the boat to crash into. Now build the first few steps with side walls.

2

Continue to build more steps, each 3 blocks wide (excluding the walls). You can save on building blocks by leaving out the outside lower corners of each step. Just don't leave any holes on the inside of the slide to ensure it is watertight when you add water.

3

How high is enough? 20 steps is good enough for a fun ride but you can keep going if you want. Now build a wide platform on top and place a safety fence around the edges. This may be a good time to eat a snack. You did bring a snack, right?

4

The waterslide looks a little bland. Let's make it cooler by placing a stone slab and a torch on top of each side wall. Do this for every step, from top to bottom. Depending on where your slide is, you could add other blocks to match its surroundings.

HOW TO BUILD A
WATERSLIDE

5

Pour 3 buckets of water on the 3 rear blocks of the highest step. The water should flow all the way to the bottom. Then cut a hole in the platform floor and drop a gravel block through. This will mark where you should stand to build a column for the ladder.

6

Standing on the gravel, facing the slide, place two wood planks in front of you and hop onto them. Jump up and place another one under your feet, and continue this until you reach the platform. Finally, place ladders on the column and install a trapdoor over the hole.

7

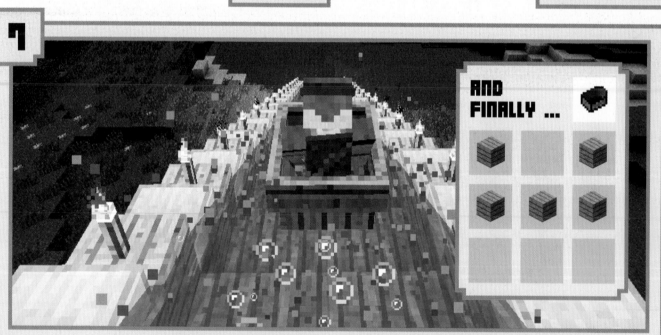

AND FINALLY ...

Now for the fun part! Place a boat on the waterslide and hop in! For best results, put the boat in the centre of the slide and let gravity do the rest.

And why not try a night run; the slide will look great with your torches lit. But do watch out for creepers ... they love waterslides!

HOW TO BUILD A
MOB SPAWNER TRAP
BY PAUL SOARES JR

T his is a great, if dangerous, way of gathering mobs for collecting supplies and gaining experience!

DIFFICULTY ☐☐☐

CONSTRUCTION MATERIALS

1

Find a dungeon. A skeleton dungeon is ideal as it will have lots of arrows and bones. Defeat the dungeon, but do not destroy the spawner! Instead, simply deactivate it by placing lots of torches in the room, which prevents monsters from spawning while you build the trap. If you can't find a spawner, search for mob spawner seeds on the internet.

2

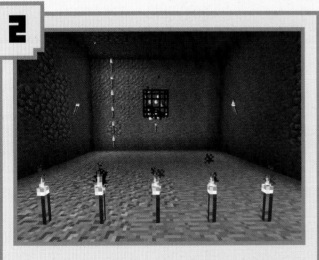

Dig 4 blocks to the sides of the spawner and two blocks down so the finished dimensions will be 9 x 9 x 6. The spawner will be floating in the centre of the room with torches placed all around it. Creepy, hey? But if you think that's creepy, just you wait until those torches go out and the monsters start to spawn!

3

You're going to need several buckets of water so it's a good idea to make an infinite water source. Find a suitable area outside of the dungeon and dig a 2 x 2 square pit. Pour two water buckets in diagonally opposite corners. Now you can refill the buckets from the pool and it will never run out of water.

HOW TO BUILD A
MOB SPAWNER TRAP

4

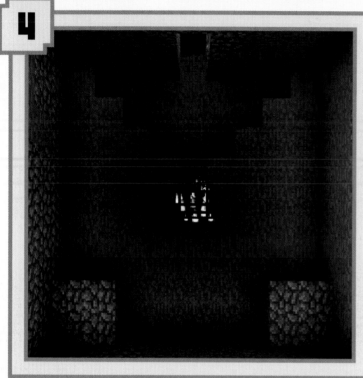

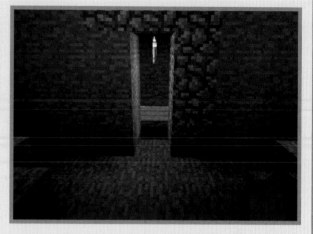

Build one-block-high corner stones in 2 corners. Then dig a one block drop-off in a funnel shape at the opposite end of the room. At the end of the funnel, dig into the wall 2 back and 3 high. Place a sign in the back with parting words for the doomed monsters!

5

In front of the sign, dig the chute down 4 blocks. At the bottom turn to your left and make a 2 x 6 chamber (2 blocks wide beneath the chute and 6 blocks in length running away from the chute). Make the far end of the chamber 1 block deeper and place a pair of signs, facing each other, on the walls at the drop-off. They will later save you from a watery death!

6

At the lower, far end of the chamber, away from the chute, dig your way up and put a ladder in place so that you'll be able to climb out to safety when the mob spawner trap is in action. If all has gone well, you should come out directly back into the spawner room! Are you in the right place? Great, let's get going with the finishing touches.

7

Back below, place glass blocks around the bottom of the chute in the chamber as shown. Just be sure not to block the chute itself. Next, place a single cobblestone block against the back wall on the floor adjacent to the chute.

8

Pour two water buckets on the back wall above the cobblestone block to fill the pool and create the delivery flow. Next, place two glass blocks just above the water drop-off point to trap those dangerous monsters in the pool you've just created!

9

Back in the spawner room, with full buckets, place torches on the floor and remove any torches from the walls and spawner. Pour the water buckets on the two corner stones and run for the exit. Whatever you do, DO NOT go down the chute! Block off the doorway behind you as you leave and head back down to the chamber.

10

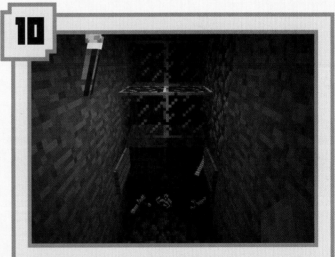

Once in the chamber, wait for monsters to spawn and drop into the dunk pool. Once there you can simply wait at the bottom and collect the loot as they drown. Alternatively, you can attack their feet and kill them for experience orbs.

Video tutorial by Paul Soares
bit.ly/10x4fV0

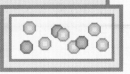

HOW TO BUILD A
SLIDING PISTON DOOR

BY NICK FARWELL

Redstone may seem daunting, but by following this simple step-by-step guide you'll be in full control with this amazing sliding door!

CONSTRUCTION MATERIALS

PISTON

STICKY PISTON

NICK FARWELL

Nick Farwell of CNB Minecraft, is a redstone wizard. His builds include digital clocks and combination locks!

1

Begin by deciding where you would like your sliding piston doorway and then make some space to fit your pistons. The door frame should be 3 blocks high and 3 blocks wide, leaving a 2 x 1 gap in the middle to form the space for the door.

2

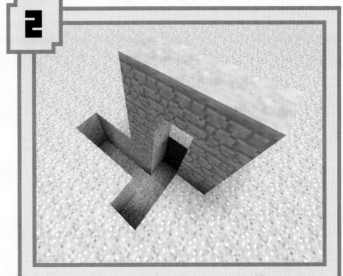

Once you have the doorway in place you will have to do some digging. Starting from the doorway, dig a 2 deep T-shaped trench into the ground. It should be 3 x 4. The 3 being perpendicular to the doorway, the 4 being parallel with it.

3

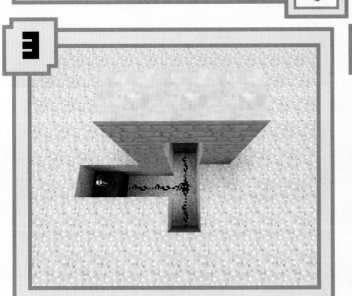

The next step is to place 5 pieces of redstone dust at the bottom of the trench, leaving one gap. The space that does not have redstone placed on should be filled with a block with a redstone torch on top.

4

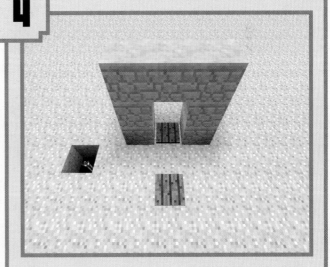

The trench with all the workings in it can now be covered up with sand and 2 pressure plates placed as shown above. When the door is finished, this will allow you to open and close the door from either side – nice! Time for a snack?

HOW TO BUILD A
SLIDING PISTON DOOR

5

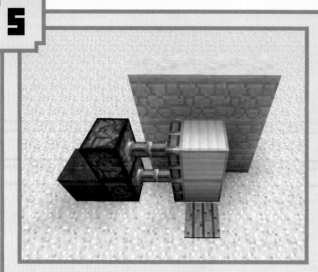

Place a block on top of the redstone torch and put redstone dust on top of it. Then place 2 sticky pistons, one on top of the other, on their side facing towards the doorway, with 2 blocks of stone in front.

6

The 2 blocks you have just placed will form the part of the door you will see sliding, so as far as visitors are concerned, the actual door. The image shows the finished doorway with the door closed. Simply step on either of the pressure plates to open it.

7

Finally, make sure that your doorway is sufficiently covered so that all you can see are the sliding blocks and the pressure plates for activating the door. Just where you use your door is up to you!

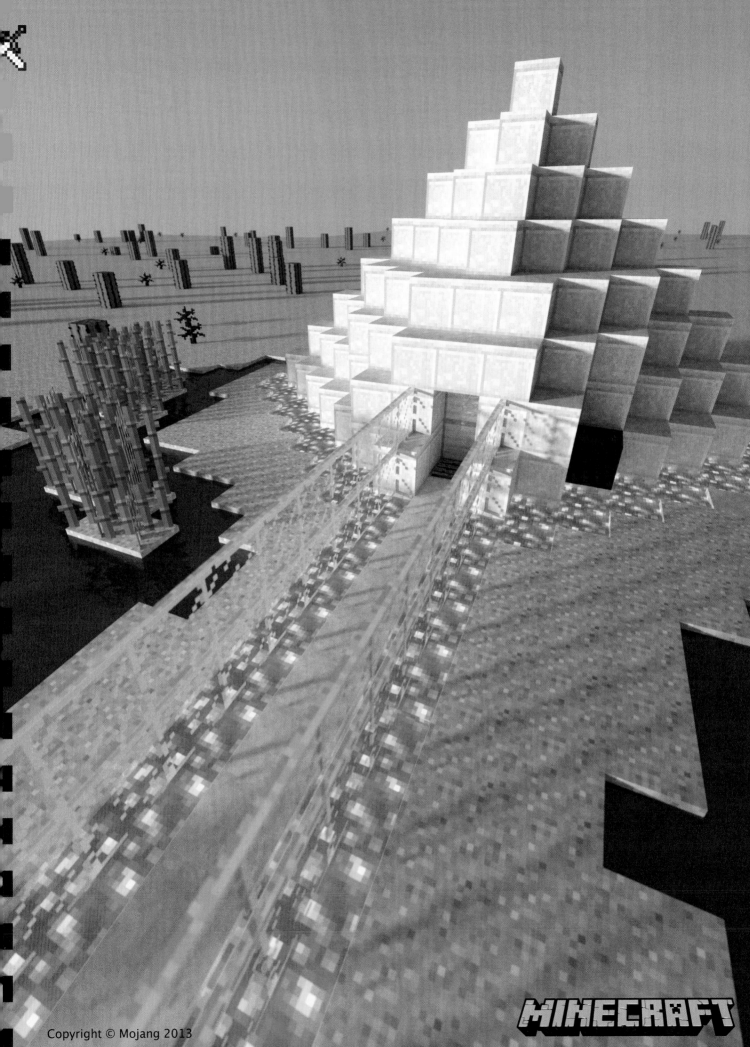

MINECRAFT

BLOCKS
ARE
BEST

DESIGN YOUR OWN
SKINS

Steve's a nice guy – but if you're finding him a bit ... how to put it nicely ... generic, why not have a go at creating your own skins? If you need some inspiration, take a look at these!

MOJANG

BUILD YOUR OWN
DIRT BLOCK

Use your Minecraft crafting skills to get crafting in the real world and make your own dirt block and creeper! Cut out these nets (templates). The black lines show where you cut, the dotted lines where you fold and the cream tabs are where to put glue. You can photocopy these pages and create as many as you like!

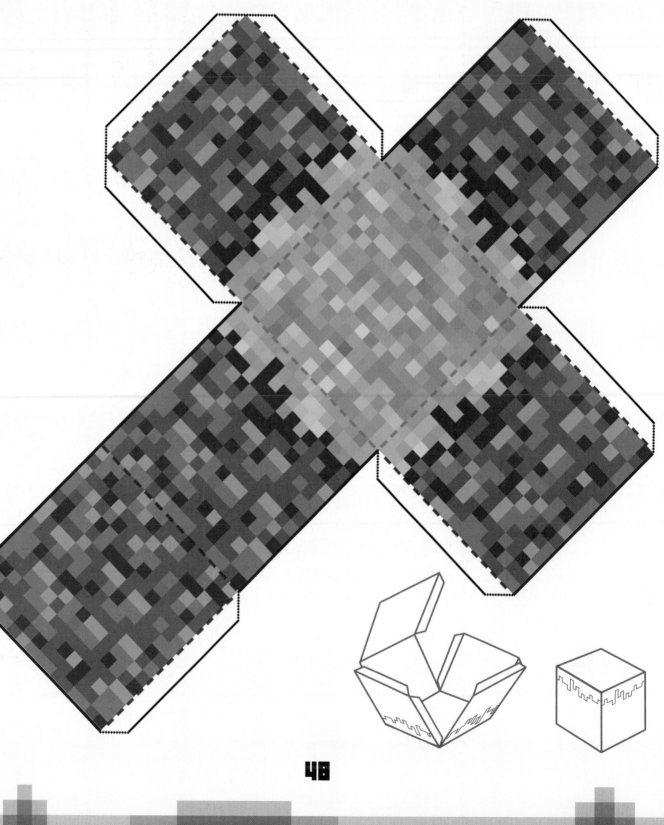

CRAFT YOUR OWN
CREEPER

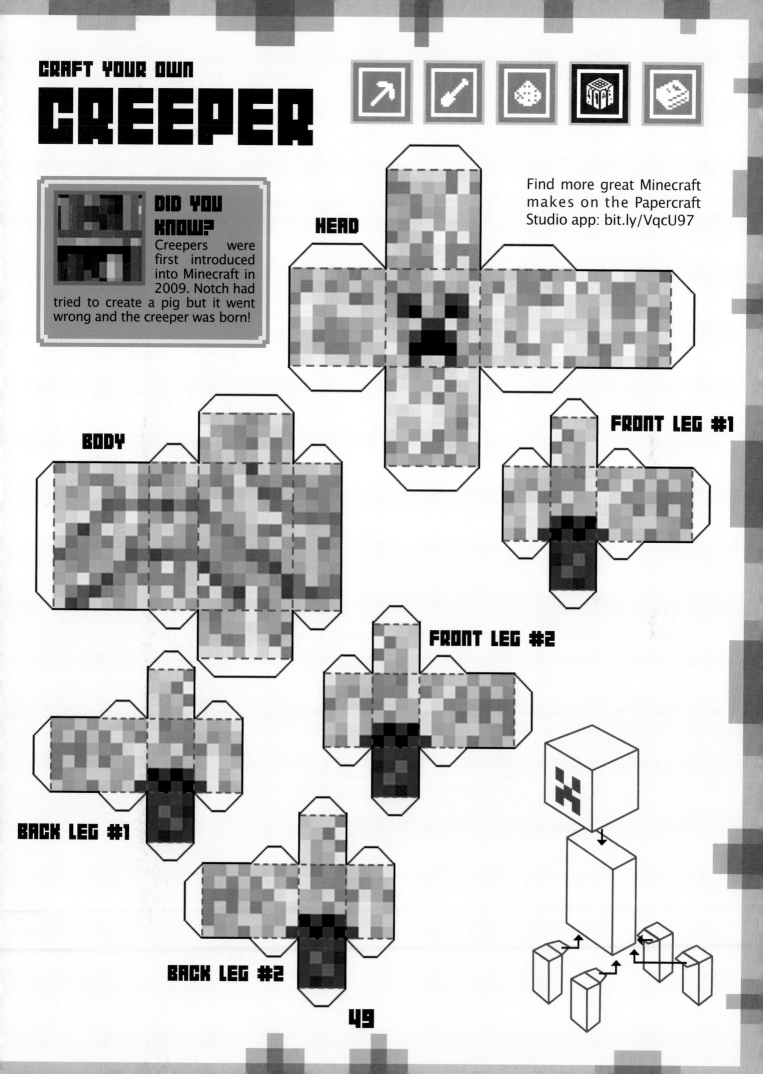

DID YOU KNOW?
Creepers were first introduced into Minecraft in 2009. Notch had tried to create a pig but it went wrong and the creeper was born!

Find more great Minecraft makes on the Papercraft Studio app: bit.ly/VqcU97

HEAD

BODY

FRONT LEG #1

FRONT LEG #2

BACK LEG #1

BACK LEG #2

49

SPIDER WEB

Help Steve get from one side of the web to the other – having 'stacks' of fun along the way! Each part of the journey, whether it be horizontal, vertical or diagonal, must add up to a stack – 64. The first three have been done for you. Good luck!

KNOCK KNOCK

Minecraft isn't for the faint-hearted. Keep annoying brothers and sisters and nervous mothers out of the mining zone with this ore-some door hanger.

STRICTLY NO CREEPERS ALLOWED

STRICTLY NO CREEPERS ALLOWED

WELCOME

TO

'S

SPAWN POINT

DID YOU KNOW?
You can create a new spawn point by crafting a bed and sleeping there. It only works if you sleep in it though!

CODE BREAKING

Use the SGA (Standard Galactic Alphabet) to decode this message from Mojang's lead developer, Jeb.

DID YOU KNOW?
The SGA, created by Tom Hall, was first used in the Commander Keen games. It was chosen as the language in Minecraft for the cryptic runes in enchantments.

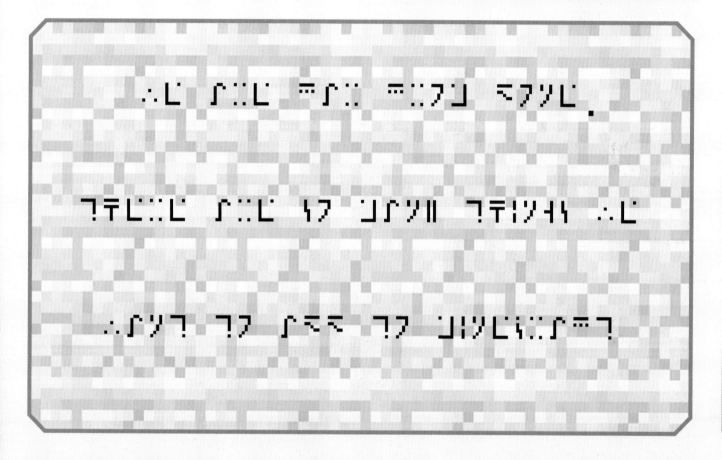

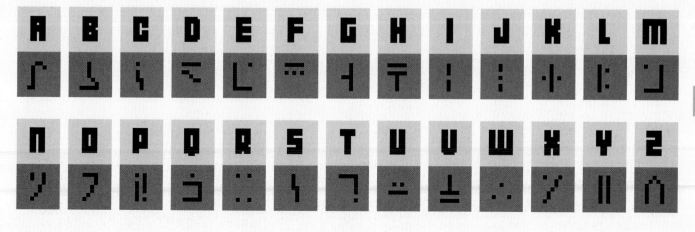

53

Answer on page 66.

SSSS ... BOOM!

There are 15 words hidden in this explosive grid. They all begin with the letter s! 5 are blocks, 4 are hostile mobs, 3 are enchantments, 2 are tools and 1 is a biome. Words can read up, down, forwards or backwards.

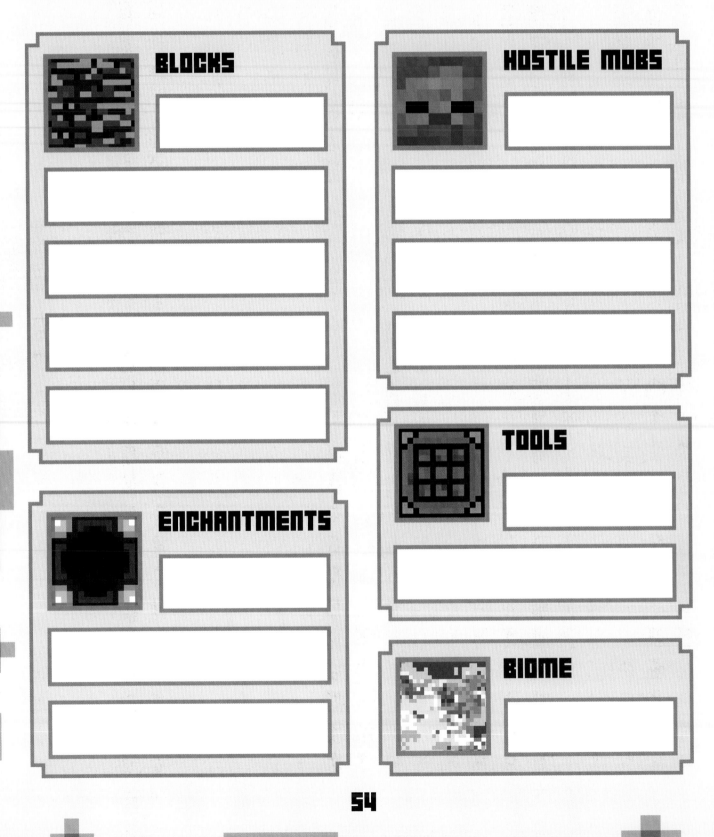

BLOCKS

HOSTILE MOBS

TOOLS

ENCHANTMENTS

BIOME

```
S U G J U N F I S L U E R Y H C U O T K L I S
N M S H E A R S P X U M N W E A S O U W I B L
Q C M L I M S L C R E S B R E S G I Y A N S O
S G S K L E O T N S A S O O U E A S R W A P S
P E S L K M O N P S O R X E T I M S N T S H B
O P L E G         L O M B O       L S U O S
N J O X C         M O L I O       M L U N H
G S O R M         A S T K B       P X H X O
E E I D E         E M I L S       J M S L U
V A L S O R S C E         S A N D S T O N E
R Y I S G O I G N         O F S S G J U N L
H O J O M S L             O E L U L P C
N M N T Y P U             F K P W S M E
E W O R I S E             E D W O A J B
S M T S I M R             P O S O N S G
A B E U E H F     N H E S O     T B S O D E S
B O L G S N I     T O S G H     Y I S S T O N
R R E D I P S H R M S W O C L O E F E D J M Q
N I K W A M H P U S O R E D T E S L N C Y B Y
U B S E R N G O E T I M S N S G E U P R W B E
H J U F N Q E S W R E P A H A N W A R T B P A
G R S D E U H E R M O L D E S R N O A S G P I
S P I H H J O R P B A R U W U R K S H O M P H
R E H M O B S T S T O N E B R I C K S O W Y E
P K E H M J W E A S S O M S E U C S E P Y M J
S I L E W R S H H O P M W K S I H L O S O A I
A N S T I C K Y P I S T O N T D A S S I U N D
```

Answers on page 66.

MINECRAFT MAPPING

Fill in the gaps below and then use the grid reference to position the answers on the map to create a crossword. The grid reference gives you the position of the first letter of the word. Some of the words read across and some down. One has been done for you.

ACROSS

<u>I R O N</u> is a commonly found ore used to make tools and armour. (58, 91)

_ _ _ _ _ _ _ become hostile when the player looks at them. (53, 88)

The _ _ _ _ _ _ is the hellish dimension in Minecraft. (53,86)

Minecraft is a _ _ _ _ box game. (53, 81)

The mobile version of Minecraft is called the _ _ _ _ _ _ edition. (53, 84)

Markus Persson is aka _ _ _ _ _ . (52, 90)

A _ _ _ _ _ _ drops ink sacs when killed. (51, 92)

DOWN

The creatures in Minecraft are known as _ _ _ _ . (51, 95)

The company that owns Minecraft is called _ _ _ _ _ _ . (60, 92)

'When _ _ _ _ fly' is the achievement you get for riding a passive mob. (53, 84)

A _ _ _ _ _ _ _ _ is a player that sets out to damage other players' creations. (57, 89)

A block capable of pushing most blocks is called a _ _ _ _ _ _ . (54, 93)

A texture that is placed onto a player or mob is called a _ _ _ _ . (58, 93)

Obsidian pillars are found in the _ _ _. (55,82)

DID YOU KNOW?
In mapping, the x co-ordinate (the horizontal) is always before the y co-ordinate (the vertical).

Answers on page 66.

A-MAZE-ING

Those pesky zombie pigmen have stolen your precious chest of diamonds and gold! Can you get it back? You'll have to find the portal first and teleport yourself to the Nether – it's the only way across.

PC/Mac users: want to try this out in Minecraft for real? You can download it from minecraft.egmont.co.uk

START

Answer on page 66.

IT'S TIME TO PLAY
RIDE THE PIG

Jump on your pig and race your friends through the Nether to the End.

YOU WILL NEED:

- 1 counter each
  (a coin or button will do)
- 1 dice
- pencils and paper to keep
  a note of your health

Place the counters on the spawn point. Take turns to throw the dice and move your pig through the game. Each player starts with full health (20). If it drops to 0 you die and respawn at the spawn point with full health.

If you land on the same square as an opponent, take them on with a dice roll contest. The player with the lowest dice roll takes 10 damage.

May the best pig win!

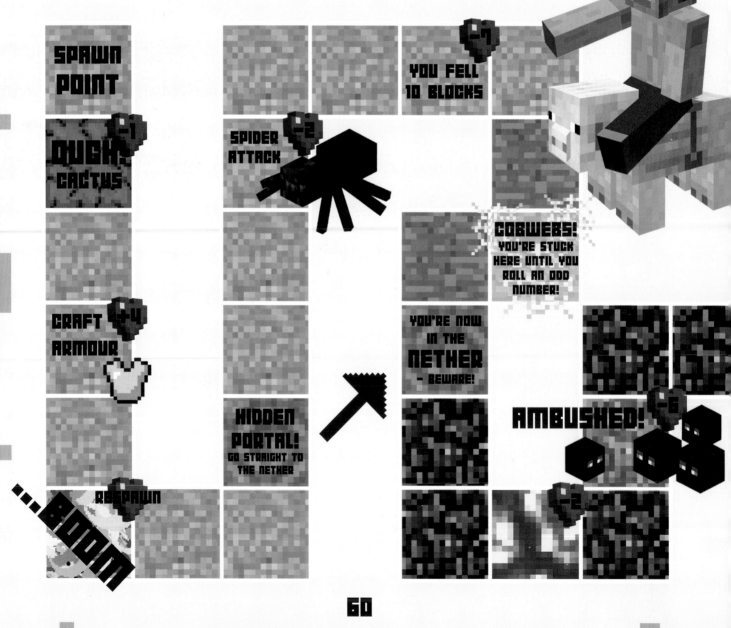

SPAWN POINT

OUCH! -1 - CACTUS

SPIDER ATTACK -2

CRAFT ARMOUR +4

RESPAWN

...BOOM

HIDDEN PORTAL! GO STRAIGHT TO THE NETHER

YOU FELL 10 BLOCKS -7

COBWEBS! YOU'RE STUCK HERE UNTIL YOU ROLL AN ODD NUMBER!

YOU'RE NOW IN THE NETHER - BEWARE!

AMBUSHED! -6

-2

BREWED A POTION

+5

-2

-2

-6

BLAZE ATTACK

-2

YOU GOT SLIMED

-4

ANGERED A ZOMBIE PIGMAN!

-9

POISONED! -1 HEALTH EVERY TURN

-1

PIG NEEDS A REST

MISS A TURN

DUCK!

-4

RESPAWN

ENDER DRAGON KNOCKED YOU OUT OF THE WORLD

FINISH

ROLL A 6 TO KILL THE ENDER DRAGON AND WIN!

ENDERMAN ATTACK

-7

ENDERMAN ATTACK

-7

BBQ TIME

+5

BLOCK-BUSTER

It's the ultimate challenge – identify each of these blocks and write the name in the space provided. There are 153 different blocks in Minecraft. How well do you know them all?

1 _ _ _ _ _ _ _

2 _ _ _ _ _

3 _ _ _ _ _ _

4 _ _ _ _ _ _ _ _ _ _

5 _ _ _ _ _ _

6 _ _ _

7 _ _ _ _ _ _ _ _ _ _ _

8 _ _ _ _ _ _ _

9 _ _ _ _

10 _ _ _ _ _ _

11 _ _ _ _ _ _ _ _ _ _

12 _ _ _ _ _ _ _ _ _ _ _

13 _ _ _ _ _

14 _ _ _ _ _ - _ - _ _ _ _ _ _ _

15 _ _ _ _ _ _

16 _ _ _ _ _ _ _ _ _

17 _ _ _ _ _ _ _ _ _ _ _ _ _ _

18 _ _ _ _ _ _ _ _ _ _ _ _ _ _

19 _ _ _ _ _ _ _ _ _

20 _ _ _ _

21 _ _ _ _ _ _ _ _ _ _ _

22 _ _ _ _ _ _ _ _ _ _

23 _ _ _ _ _ _

24 _ _ _ _ _ _ _ _ _

25 _ _ _ _ _ _ _ _ _ _

62

26 _ _ _ _ _ _ _ _ _

37 _ _ _ _ _ _ _ _ _ _ _ _ _ _

27 _ _ _ _ _ _

38 _ _ _ _ _ _ _

28 _ _ _ _ _ _ _ _

39 _ _ _ _ _ _ _ _ _ _ _ _ _

29 _ _ _ _ _ _ _ _ _ _ _ _ _

40 _ _ _ _ _ _ _

30 _ _ _ _ _ _ _ _ _

41 _ _ _ _ _ _ _

31 _ _ _ _ _ _ _ _ _

42 _ _ _ _ _ _ _ _ _ _ _ _ _ _

32 _ _ _ _ _ _ _ _ _ _ _ _ _ _

43 _ _ _ _ _ _

33 _ _ _ _ _ _ _

44 _ _ _ _ _ _ _

34 _ _ _ _ _ _ _ _ _

45 _ _ _ _ _ _ _

35 _ _ _ _ _ _ _ _ _

46 _ _ _ _ _ _ _ _ _

36 _ _ _ _ _

47 _ _ _ _ _ _ _ _ _

In each block name there is a highlighted letter. Put them into the spaces below to spell out this secret message of good advice.

_ _ _ _ _ _ _ _ _ _ _ _ _ _ _ _ _ _ _ _ _ _' _ _ _
1 2 3 4 5 6 7   8 9 10   11 12 13 14 15 16 17 18 19 20 21 22   23 24 25

_ _ _ _ _ _ _ _ _ _ _ _ _ _ _ _ _ _ _ _ _ _ _!
26 27 28 29 30 31 32 33 34 35 36 37 38 39 40 41 42 43 44 45 46 47

Answers on page 66.

FINAL WORDS FROM JEB

We never expected Minecraft to get this big! Thanks for building, crafting, creating, producing and exploring. You are responsible for the awesome community that exists today and we're extremely proud to have you as players. Minecraft is far from done! If you continue to enjoy our game, we'll continue to work on it!

ANSWERS

Page 50: Spider Web

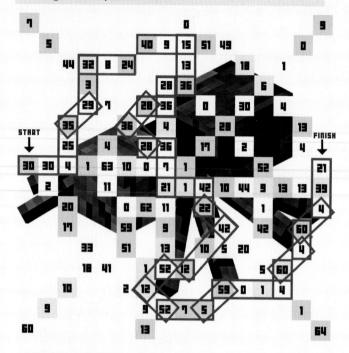

Pages 56-57: Minecraft Mapping

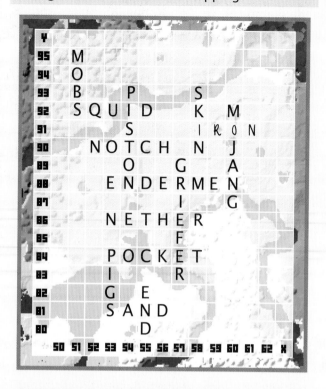

Page 53: Code Breaking

The code reads: **We are far from done. There are so many things we want to add to Minecraft.**

Pages 54-55: SSSS ... BOOM!

```
S V G J U N F I S L U E R Y H C U O T K L I S
N M S H E A R S P X U M N W E A S O U W I B L
Q C M L I M S L C R E S B R E S G I Y A N S O
S G S K L E O T N S A S O O V E A S R W A P S
P E S L K M O N P S O R X E T I M S N T S H B
P O P L E G       L O M B O         L S U O S
N J O X C         M O L I O         M L U N H
G S O R M         A S T K B         P X H X O
E E I D E         E M I L S         J M S L U
U A L S O R S C E         S A N D S T O N E
R Y I S G O I G N         O F S S G J U N L
H O J O M S L             D E L U L P C
N M N T Y P U             F K P W S M E
E W O R I S E             E D W O A J B
S M T S I M A             P O S O N S G
A B E U E H F       N H E S O     T B S O D E S
B O L G S N I       T O S G H     Y I S S T O N
R R E D I P S H A M S W O C L O E F E D J M Q
N I K W A M H P U S O A E D T E S L N C Y B Y
U B S E A N G O E T I M S N S G E U P R W B E
H J U F N Q E S W R E P A H A N W A R T B P A
G R S D E U H E R M O L D E S R N O A S G P I
S P I H H J O R P B A A U W U R K S H O M P H
R E H M O B S T S T O N E B R I C K S D W Y E
P X E H M J W E A S S D M S E U G S E P Y M J
S I L E W R S H H O P M W K S I H L O S O A I
A N S T I C K Y P I S T O N T O A S S I U N O
```

Pages 58-59: A-maze-ing

Pages 62-63: Block-buster

1. Cactus
2. Lava
3. Glass
4. Mycelium
5. Anvil
6. TNT
7. Glowstone
8. Gravel
9. Clay
10. Melon
11. Mob spawner
12. Diamond ore
13. Sand
14. Jack-o-lantern
15. Chest
16. Iron ore
17. Nether quartz
18. Crafting table
19. End stone
20. Ice
21. Stone brick
22. Bookshelf
23. Dirt
24. Pink wool
25. Grass block
26. Dispenser
27. Leaves
28. Furnace
29. Sticky piston
30. Obsidian
31. Soul sand
32. Glowstone lamp
33. Beacon
34. Moss stone
35. Note block
36. Snow
37. Redstone block
38. Bedrock
39. Daylight sensor
40. Bricks
41. Sponge
42. Chiseled stone
43. Water
44. Dropper
45. Hopper
46. Lime wool
47. Pumpkin

The secret message is:

**CALLING ALL MINECRAFTERS,
DIG DEEP BUT NOT STRAIGHT DOWN!**

READER SURVEY

we'd like to know what you think about your Minecraft Annual.

Ask a grown-up to help you fill in this form and post it to the address at the end by 28th February 2014, or you can fill in the survey online at www.egmont.co.uk/minecraftsurvey2014.

One lucky reader will win £150 of book tokens!
Five runners-up will win a £25 book token each.

1 WHO BOUGHT THIS MINECRAFT ANNUAL?

☐ Me
☐ Parent/guardian
☐ Grandparent
☐ Other (please specify)

2 WHY DID THEY BUY IT?

☐ Christmas present
☐ Birthday present
☐ Other (please specify)

_____

_____

3 WHAT ARE YOUR FAVOURITE PARTS OF THE MINECRAFT ANNUAL?

Game information	☐ Really like	☐ Like	☐ Don't like
Minecraft builds	☐ Really like	☐ Like	☐ Don't like
Things to make & do	☐ Really like	☐ Like	☐ Don't like
Puzzles	☐ Really like	☐ Like	☐ Don't like
Games	☐ Really like	☐ Like	☐ Don't like

4 DO YOU THINK THE MINECRAFT BUILDS ARE TOO DIFFICULT, TOO EASY OR ABOUT RIGHT?

☐ Too difficult
☐ Too easy
☐ About right

5 DO YOU THINK THE PUZZLES ARE TOO HARD, TOO EASY OR ABOUT RIGHT?

☐ Too hard
☐ Too easy
☐ About right

6 WHAT ARE YOUR FAVOURITE THINGS ABOUT MINECRAFT?

1 _____

2 _____

3 _____

7 WHICH OTHER ANNUALS DO YOU LIKE?

1 _____

_____

2 _____

_____

3 _____

_____

8 WHAT IS YOUR FAVOURITE . . .

1 ... app or website?

_____

2 ... console game?

_____

3 ... magazine?

_____

4 ... book?

_____

9 WHAT ARE YOUR FAVOURITE TV PROGRAMMES?

1 _____

_____

2 _____

_____

3 _____

_____

10 WOULD YOU LIKE TO GET THE MINECRAFT ANNUAL AGAIN NEXT YEAR?

☐ Yes   ☐ No

Why? _____

_____

_____

_____

THANK YOU! (Please ask your parent/guardian to complete)

Child's name: _____ Age: _____ Boy / Girl

Parent/guardian name: _____

Parent/guardian signature: _____

Parent/guardian email address: _____

Daytime telephone number: _____

**PLEASE CUT OUT AND POST TO:
MINECRAFT READER SURVEY
EGMONT UK LIMITED
THE YELLOW BUILDING
1 NICHOLAS ROAD
LONDON W11 4AN**

GOOD LUCK!

☐ **PLEASE SEND ME THE EGMONT MONTHLY CATCH-UP NEWSLETTER.**

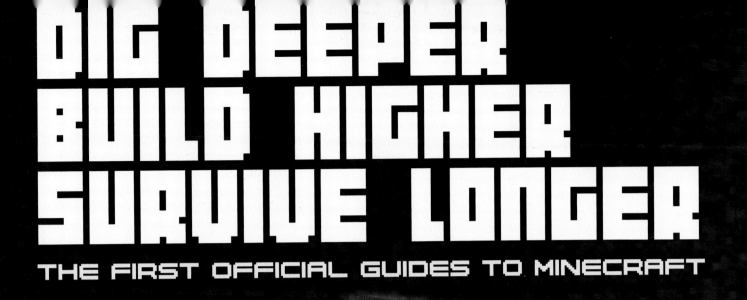

DIG DEEPER
BUILD HIGHER
SURVIVE LONGER

THE FIRST OFFICIAL GUIDES TO MINECRAFT

OUT NOW!

COMING NOV 2013

AVAILABLE ONLINE AND IN ALL GOOD BOOKSHOPS

MINECRAFT.EGMONT.CO.UK

EGMONT